THE STARTUP SQUAD

YOU'RE THE BOSS

A KID'S ULTIMATE GUIDE TO STARTING YOUR OWN BUSINESS

By **Brian Weisfeld** and **Bonnie Bader**

PHILOMEL

PHILOMEL
An imprint of Penguin Random House LLC
1745 Broadway, New York, New York 10019

First published in the United States of America by Philomel,
an imprint of Penguin Random House LLC, 2024

Visit us online at PenguinRandomHouse.com.

Library of Congress Cataloging-in-Publication Data is available.

ISBN 9780593528365

3 5 7 9 10 8 6 4 2

Printed in the United States of America

BVG

Cover and chapter header illustrations by Sydney Day
Design by Monique Sterling
Text set in Franziska Pro

This is a work of nonfiction. Some names and identifying details have been changed.

For help with the business content, special thanks to Sara Heston, Associate Director,
Center for Entrepreneurial Studies at the Stanford Graduate School of Business
(and Claire!).

CONTENTS

For more business resources and downloadable worksheets, visit
youretheboss.com/mybiz

INTRODUCTION

When Mikaila Ulmer was four years old, she was stung by a bee. And believe it or not, less than a week later she was stung again! (Not by the same bee, of course.) The stings hurt, and Mikaila became frightened of bees.

But instead of hiding from them, Mikaila started researching those flying—and sometimes stinging—insects. She became fascinated. Mikaila learned that some bees make honey and that bees are a very important part of our ecosystem. But she also learned that bees are endangered and that without bees, there would be a lot fewer flowers, fruits, and vegetables in the world.

Around the same time, Mikaila's parents encouraged her to create a product for two children's business fairs: the Acton Children's Business Fair and Lemonade Day. What should she make? Mikaila thought and thought. When she received a cookbook from her great-granny Helen that included a recipe for flaxseed lemonade, she wondered if she should use that recipe. Great-granny's lemonade sounded delicious . . . but could she put an original spin on the recipe to make it her own?

Then Mikaila had an idea. What if she created something that brought awareness to the fact that bees are endangered *and* used her great-granny's recipe at the same time? So Mikaila added some honey to Great-Granny's recipe. The lemonade tasted delicious! And that was the very moment her business was born.

Mikaila started selling her lemonade at the business fairs and from a stand outside her home in Austin, Texas. She learned how to save some money from her business and how to create a budget for buying supplies. She donated a portion of her profits to organizations that were working to protect honeybees, and she came up with the business slogan "Buy a Bottle . . . Save a Bee."

Today, Mikaila runs a successful business that continues to grow and grow. By the time she was fourteen years old, she'd sold more than a million bottles of her award-winning lemonade, Me & the Bees Lemonade, in supermarkets across the nation. Plus, Mikaila has an entire team working for her, including her mom! And when Mikaila is not busy making lemonade, she is speaking to other kids about being an entrepreneur and how to help the bees (of course!). She even published her own book: *Bee Fearless: Dream Like a Kid.*

Of course, starting and maintaining a business isn't always as smooth as honey. Mikaila had several challenges along the way, but by working hard and seeing opportunities instead of problems, she succeeded. And you can, too!

Read on to create your own recipe for success . . .

1

WHAT IS YOUR WHY?

Have you ever had your eye on that special something, say a phone or a new bike, but didn't have the money to pay for it? And when you asked your parents or guardians to help you pay for that item, they said no? At six years old, Cory Nieves already knew what that's like. He was tired of taking the bus to school. His dream was to buy a car for his mom. But how could he make enough money?

First he sold hot chocolate in his hometown of Englewood, New Jersey. Then he started a lemonade stand. He really found his calling when he set out on a quest to make the perfect chocolate chip cookie with organic ingredients. With the help of his mother (yes, it's okay to ask for help!), he created Mr. Cory's Cookies. Soon he expanded his business to make double dark, oatmeal raisin, and sugar cookies. Today, Mr. Cory's Cookies can be purchased online, and they're shipped all over the country.

Or have you ever gone shopping for something and been unable to find the right thing, no matter how long and how hard you looked? That happened to **Kamaria Warren** from Atlanta, Georgia, when she went shopping for invitations for her eighth birthday party. She and her mom didn't see anything that represented brown and Black girls. Instead of settling for something they didn't want, they created their own invitations and party supplies. And when that got a good response, they turned it into a business, Brown Girls Stationery.

Photo by Shaunice Sasser

Cory, Kamaria, and lots of other real kids show how it's possible for anyone to start a business. Even you!

Whoa—that might seem really, really hard. It's tough for anyone to start a business, let alone a young person, right? But in fact, lots of successful business owners started businesses when they were young:

- When businessman and star of *Shark Tank* Mark Cuban was twelve, he asked his dad to buy him a pair of expensive sneakers. His dad said no, but a friend of his dad's offered Mark an opportunity to earn some money by selling garbage bags. Knowing that everyone in his neighborhood used garbage bags, Mark went door-to-door, convincing his neighbors to buy from him. And since his price for the bags was lower than the price at the local store, many people did!

- Charles Schwab, who today is a billionaire, wanted to make some extra money when he was young. His first job was collecting walnuts and selling them for five dollars a bag. Later he raised chickens in his backyard and sold the eggs.

- Lorrie King, the cofounder of the beauty line Caire Beauty, always wanted to stand out and have people recognize her as being smart. In fourth grade she started selling homemade sandwiches to the teachers at her school. Lorrie loved being recognized as a young entrepreneur and went on to become a successful businesswoman.

It's never too early to start your own business. It can be a service you provide (like babysitting or lawn mowing) or a product you sell (like cookies or party supplies). You may want to start a business to make money to buy something you want, like Cory or Mark Cuban. Or you may want to start a business to create something there is a need for, like Kamaria. You might also want to start a business to make money to donate to a cause or charity, like Mikaila.

On a separate piece of paper, write down some reasons why you want to start a business. Is there something special you want to buy? Is there a product you think the world needs? Here's an example:

WHY I WANT TO START A BUSINESS

I want to make money to buy a tablet.

I want to make money to buy a present for my mom's birthday.

I want to start a business with my best friend so we can have fun working together!

I want to start a business so I can donate money to the animal shelter.

STARTUP SECRET

When you create your own business, product, or service, you are called an *entrepreneur*. An entrepreneur is not afraid of taking risks and knows how to turn problems into business opportunities.

Starting a business will teach you how to:
- be a leader
- feel more comfortable taking healthy risks and talking to people
- see opportunities when everyone else sees a problem
- keep on going during hard times
- be organized and responsible
- manage your time

And you won't just be using these skills in your business; these are skills that you will use in your everyday life! For example, being organized and responsible and mastering time management can help you get your homework done more efficiently. Being a leader could help you become captain of your sports team. And becoming comfortable with taking risks might enable you to attempt those gymnastics moves you've feared trying.

Being an entrepreneur is about taking chances, making mistakes, and then dusting yourself off and starting all over again. You can do it! Read on to find out how.

2

IDENTIFY YOUR INTERESTS

Now that you know *why* you want to start a business, it's time to figure out *what* business you will create. Obviously, you wouldn't want to start a business doing something you don't enjoy, so first figure out what you *like* to do. What are your interests?

Think about what you like to do in your spare time. Read? Play sports? Make videos on your phone? Teach your dog tricks? All these things are your **interests**—if they didn't interest you, you wouldn't do them!

On a separate piece of paper, write down a list of your interests. Here's an example:

MY INTERESTS

Reading

Watching videos

Gaming

Biking

Baking

Taking care of my dog

Hanging out with my friends

If you are stuck and aren't able to come up with a list, don't worry! Ask your friends and family to help you brainstorm some things that might appeal to you. Do they have any observations about how you choose to spend your free time? You may be surprised at what they come up with.

Is there someone in your life who you admire? A teacher? A relative? A neighbor? What do you admire about them? Perhaps they have a job or hobby that you find interesting. If so, sit down and talk with them. Maybe you will find that what they do is something you want to pursue as well.

Take a look at what you wrote down. Is there anything on this list that you are good at (or think that you can become good at)? This is a **skill**. A skill is the ability to perform a task well. Sometimes we ignore our own skills because they seem so easy to us. For example, you might be able to help your parents or grandparents figure stuff out on their devices. While this may be no big deal to you, it is a skill because not everyone can do it. Make notes on your interests list about which things you are skilled at. Here's an example:

Reading—I'm pretty good at reading, but not sure it's something I'm particularly talented at.

Watching videos—I'm pretty good at this, but I wouldn't say it's a skill!

Gaming—I'm pretty skilled, but not an expert.

Biking—I like doing this for fun and exercise, but it's not really a skill.

Baking—Everyone compliments what I make, so I think I'm pretty SKILLED.

Taking care of my dog—I'm the best in my family at taking care of my dog! SKILL.

Hanging out with my friends—Um, I think I'm pretty good at this . . . but not sure it's really a skill (although it might help me with my business at some point!).

Okay, now that you've uncovered some of your skills, take some time to think about your enthusiasm level.

Enthusiasm is being very interested in, or very excited about, something. How enthusiastic you are about something is a key ingredient to your success. For example, if you are skilled at caring for little kids but you don't really enjoy doing it, then you probably wouldn't want to start a babysitting business. However, if you are skilled at baking and really love to bake, then you might want to incorporate baking into your business.

STARTUP SECRET

If you are very excited about something that you have an interest in, or are skilled at, this is called having a **passion**. A passion is what you really, really like to do.

When looking for your interests, skills, and passions, it is important to do something that *you* want to do, not just something that all your friends are doing. Of course, it's possible that you and your friends have the same interests, but don't be a follower. Lead with your own heart and mind.

....

If you feel like there's something out there that you're supposed to be doing, if you have a passion for it, then stop wishing and just do it.

—Wanda Sykes, actor and author

....

★ ★ ★ STARTUP STAR ★ ★ ★

Sara Robinson's passion for sewing inspired her to form her own business. Sara learned to sew when she was seven years old. Just for fun, she started selling her handmade doll dresses on Facebook. Soon Sara added dresses for girls, along with aprons and party banners. She wanted to reach more people with her products, and that's when Sara Sews was born. Today, Sara has her own Etsy shop and a team of sewers making her designs. She sells thousands of aprons a year. Sara and her team have also sewed more than two thousand face masks and donated them to several hospitals, assisted living homes, and doctors in her home state of Georgia. You can learn more about Sara and buy her products at **ShopSaraSews.com**.

Bella Bliss Photography—Amy Johns Studios

Remember: Everyone has interests and skills. You just have to open up your eyes to find yours!

3

PICK A PROBLEM

Problems are everywhere; just look around. But instead of running and hiding from problems, run toward them—with a solution! What does this have to do with starting a business? Everything!

Entrepreneurs take problems and turn them into opportunities to start businesses. These are some inventions that solved everyday problems:

- **Problem:** It's nighttime and it's dark. But you really, really have to go to the bathroom. What can you do?

  Solution: put on a pair of LED slippers to help light your way!

- **Problem:** Your dad keeps on cutting his finger trying to slice slippery onions.

Solution: give him an instrument designed to hold the onion steady.

- **Problem:** Someone keeps eating up your favorite ice cream.

  Solution: put on an ice cream container lock, with a combination that only you know!

These everyday problems were solved by creative inventions. Is there such a problem that you can try to solve by creating a product?

One day, twenty-seven-year-old Sara Blakely put on a pair of white pants. As she stood facing the mirror, she thought it might look better if she wore a pair of tights underneath the pants. But the tights' seams made her toes feel uncomfortable. So Sara grabbed a pair of scissors and cut the feet off the tights. This was a perfect solution to her everyday problem! Sara thought others would enjoy this undergarment, too. She took her life's savings—five thousand dollars—and started a business called Spanx, which today is worth billions of dollars!

Just like Sara, Jenn Hyman and Jenny Fleiss took an everyday problem and turned it into a big business. Jenn's sister, Becky, had a wedding to go to but didn't want to spend a ton of money on a dress that she would wear only once or twice. So Jenn and Jenny (who had been brainstorming about starting a business together) came up with the idea of renting dresses for special occasions, like weddings. And so their company, Rent the Runway, was born.

Here's something that you probably don't realize was ever a problem: renting movies. The story goes that in 1997, Reed Hastings was fined forty dollars for returning a movie to a video rental store six weeks late. (In those days, people had to go to a store and pay money to rent a single movie, which came in a plastic box. Then they'd take that box home, watch the movie on their TV using a specialized device, and return the physical movie to the movie rental store. If they didn't return it within a set number of days, they were charged a fine!)

The forty-dollar late fee may not be true. But the rest definitely is. Reed and his friend Marc Randolph set up a company where people could get three DVD movies (these were discs that you put into a digital video player) per month and not be charged a late fee. The only way you could get a new movie was by sending one of your other movie rentals back. They called their company Netflix. And while Netflix has gone through its ups and downs as a business, today it is one of the most successful streamers of movies and TV shows.

If you don't immediately see an everyday problem to solve, just look around your town, school, or neighborhood.

Do your neighbors need help raking leaves in the fall or shoveling snow in the winter? Are there little kids who need babysitters? How about older people who might need help with grocery shopping or doing chores around their homes?

If you want to do some research to find a problem that you can help fix, you can consult

- Newspapers
- Websites
- Books
- People in your neighborhood, including community leaders such as politicians, teachers, and shop owners

Look for issues that interest you. Perhaps a local school is having trouble getting enough books for its students. Or you could do a search for ways to help pick up litter in your neighborhood. Try to get information from more than one source.

Communities have many, many issues that need solving. Here are some problems that you might find right in your own town:

- Too many animals up for adoption, not enough homes, and the shelters are overcrowded
- Not enough bicycle lanes or sidewalks
- Some people can't afford to buy food and are hungry
- Lots of kids have trouble learning to read

- Many older people have difficulty getting things done around the house
- Lots of garbage on the streets
- Not enough people recycle

On a separate piece of paper, make a list of some of the problems you observe in your life, your neighborhood, and the world at large, like this:

ISSUES I NOTICE

Kids have trouble getting homework done when their phones are nearby.

The local animal shelter doesn't have enough money to care for all the stray animals.

There are not enough bike lanes.

There are often really long waits to check out my favorite books from the library.

Now that you have this list, think about and research one of these issues by using some of the same kinds of sources you used before. When did this situation become a problem? What has already been done to try to help or improve this issue? What do you think you can do to help?

★★★ STARTUP STAR ★★★

When **Alina Morse** was seven years old, she went to the bank with her dad and a bank teller offered her a lollipop. While she really wanted to accept the treat, she knew from her parents that sugar was bad for her teeth. Alina asked her dad, "Why can't we make a lollipop that's *good* for your teeth?" And so they did!

Photo by Zolli Candy

With her dad, Alina created Zollipops, a delicious sugar-free lollipop that actually cleans your teeth. Their mission is to help reduce tooth decay, a problem that millions of kids across America face. Alina's business became so successful that she was featured in *Entrepreneur*, a magazine about entrepreneurship and small businesses. At age fourteen, Alina was the youngest person ever to be featured on the cover of that magazine! Alina is from a suburb of Detroit, Michigan, but her Zollipops are sold in stores all over the country and online at **Zollipops.com**.

Besides community issues, there are also global issues that you might want to help solve by starting a business. In 2007, recent college graduate Kenton Lee traveled to Nairobi, Kenya, to work at an orphanage. One day he saw a little girl walking down a road in shoes so small that a hole was cut in the front so her toes could stick out. Kenton knew that many people in her village, and in villages around the world, couldn't afford to buy kids a new pair of shoes each time their feet grew. Kenton saw this problem and had an idea: What if there was a shoe that grew along with a kid's foot?

After six years, Kenton and a group of friends created The Shoe That Grows. This shoe can expand by five sizes and is distributed to kids in need around the world.

While it might be difficult to try to address huge issues such as poverty or hunger or climate change, you could use your business to raise money for organizations that help these causes. Contributing money is not only a good thing for that organization but will make you feel good, too!

There are lots of problems in our neighborhoods and in our world. Perhaps you can start a business or create a product that will bring us one step closer to a solution!

4
IT'S AN IDEA!

N ow you have your *why.*

You know your *interests, skills,* and *passions.*

And you may even have a *problem* that you can solve by starting a business. (Although you don't always need a problem to start a business.)

It's time to get down to business—literally!—and come up with your idea.

Your mind might be swirling with possibilities. You can use any of those as a jumping-off point to start a business.

But what if your mind *isn't* swirling? What if your mind is stuck? That's okay too. It's just time to do some more brainstorming! Look again at your list of interests and skills and at your list of community issues or other problems.

Get your ideas on paper and study them.

Do not let them go to waste!

—Les Brown, motivational speaker

Now that you have your lists, it's time to mind map. On a separate piece of paper, make a mind map, like this:

MIND MAP

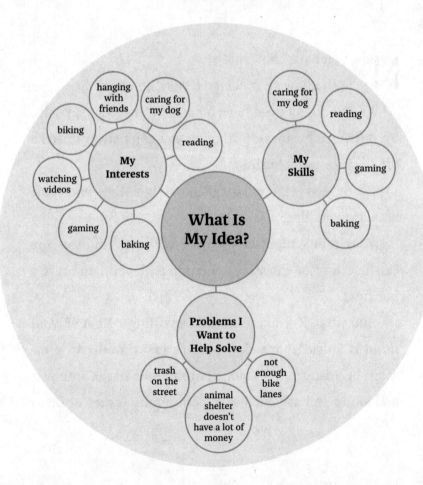

Study your mind map. Is there a business that you can develop that fits with one (or more!) of your interests or passions? Can you come up with a business idea that will help solve a problem? Your business idea doesn't have to be a passion *and* solve a problem, although it's even better if it does both.

....

Get a good idea and stay with it. Do it,
and work at it until it's done right.

—Walt Disney, animator and film producer

....

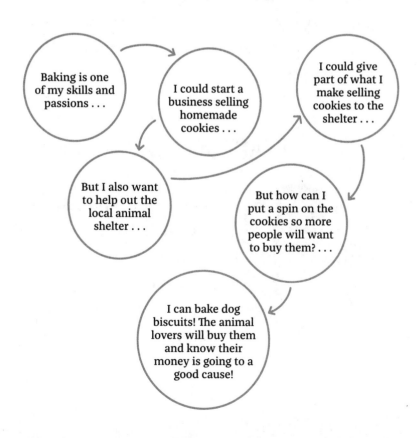

Now write down your business idea, like this:

MY BUSINESS IDEA

HOMEMADE DOG BISCUITS!

Your business doesn't have to be a totally new idea. It's okay if that business already exists; you just have to put a special spin on yours. Some entrepreneurs start businesses to improve on a product that already exists, like a better video game or a more environmentally friendly soap. For example, Steve Jobs, the cofounder of Apple, didn't invent the computer or cell phone. But he *did* make both stand out from the competition.

★ ★ ★ STARTUP STAR ★ ★ ★

Photo by Julia Scheeres

One day, **Tessa and Davia**'s mom brought them home a shampoo bar that she had purchased at the local mall. Tessa and Davia were excited to use it, but after shampooing, their hair felt sticky, and not very clean. Plus, the bar was really expensive. So, they decided to see if they could make their own shampoo bar.

After a lot of research and experimenting, the sisters created a shampoo bar that left their hair smelling and feeling great. Their bars were also a lot less expensive to make and were produced from all-natural ingredients, and no animal products. After refining the bar even more, Tessa took them to her middle school fair and they sold out! The sisters knew they were onto something and created their business, Sustainabar, in 2020.

Today, the sisters sell an entire range of zero-waste bars ranging from shampoo and conditioner to dish soap and lotion. In addition, their packaging is made from 100 percent recyclable/compostable material, such as shredded newspapers and junk mail. To date, the sisters have sold more than 9,000 bars—eliminating about 18,000 plastic bottles. Through producing Sustainabar, the sisters have eliminated over eight hundred plastic bottles (which is what similar products are sold in). Plus, they donate bars to local homeless shelters and community pantries. Sustainabar is sold on their website: **Sustainabar.net.**

> *If I have a thousand ideas and only one*
> *turns out to be good, I am satisfied.*
>
> —Alfred Nobel, benefactor of the Nobel Prize

The ideal business for you will be something that you love to do, and something that stands out from the competition. If your business is even just a little different from all the others, it will be uniquely yours. That may make people more intrigued by it and more eager to support you.

Having trouble thinking of a business to start? No worries! Start with a simple lemonade stand. Our favorite recipe is the juice of six squeezed lemons, six cups of water, and one cup of sugar. Maybe bake and sell some cookies or brownies, too. And while you're solving people's hunger and thirst, ask your customers what other needs they have that you could turn into a business.

You will want to make sure that there is a demand for your product or service. You don't want to start a business where you are the only customer! And that's exactly what we'll get into in the next chapter . . .

5

FINDING YOUR CUSTOMER

It's totally fine to start your business by selling just to your family and friends. But that isn't going to make you a lot of money! To be successful, a business needs customers. So before you invest time and energy in starting your new business, you must figure out who you will sell to.

The people who would want to buy your product are called your **target audience**. Now is the time to identify your perfect target audience and figure out why they would want to buy your product or service.

For example, if you are starting a dog-walking business, your target audience might be people who work in an office and want their dog cared for when they are not home. If you want to start a lemonade stand, your customers may be people who are in the park on a warm day or people who are thirsty after playing sports.

It is possible to have more than one target audience for your product or service. You could target your dog-walking business to pet owners who work *and* older people who can't walk their dogs as much as they would like. The more target audiences you have, the larger the number of potential customers for your business.

If you are making something for kids, such as slime, you would probably think that your target audience is kids. But would they have enough money to buy your slime? Perhaps their parents and other relatives are an additional, or even a better, target audience.

On a separate piece of paper, make a list of the different types of customers for your business and why they would want to buy what you are selling, like this:

TARGET AUDIENCE FOR MY BUSINESS

Homemade Dog Treats

TYPE OF CUSTOMER	WHY THEY'D PAY FOR MY DOG TREATS
Adult Pet Owners	They want to give healthy treats to their dogs.

Kids with Pets	They love their dogs and want to keep them healthy and happy.
Vets	They might want to buy some and give them to their dog "patients."
Dog Groomers	They can give them to the dogs they groom.
Dog Trainers	They can use them as rewards for the dogs they train.

Once you have your list of potential customers, go and chat with some of them. Tell them about your idea and see if it's something they might want, or if they have ideas on how you can improve your product or business. Your goal is to find out how your potential customers think and how they make their decisions. This is called **market research**.

MARKET RESEARCH QUESTIONS

1. Do you give your dog biscuits?

2. Which flavors do they like?

3. Which flavors don't they like?

4. How do you decide which dog biscuits to buy? Does it have to do with flavor, size, price, or a combination?

5. How much do you usually pay for biscuits?

6. Here is a sample biscuit. Would you be willing to give it to your dog and let me know if you think they liked it or not?

STARTUP SECRET

Imagine your perfect customer, like a friend or a neighbor who you think would love what you are selling. Keep that person in mind as you develop your marketing, logo, sales pitch, and more. Maybe even draw or print out a picture of that person and keep it on your wall as a reminder.

Remember, customers are the beating heart of your business. Without them, there will be no one to buy what you're selling!

6

TELLING YOUR STORY

To run a successful business, it's not enough just to create a good product. You also need potential customers to find out about it. Marketing is getting people interested in what you are selling and helping them understand why they would want or need your product or service. The best marketing incorporates a story about why you started your business or what makes your business unique. After all, you want to make your business seem so special that people can't resist buying from it!

Remember Alina Morse and her Zollipops? Her story was that she wanted to create a lollipop that was good for your teeth, and she did. Alina started her business to help prevent tooth decay. Why did you start *your* business? What do you hope to achieve? What makes your business stand out? This is all part of marketing.

Take a look at your product. Is it different from others? For example, if you are selling lemonade, what makes your lemonade different from the lemonade that the kid down the street is selling? Maybe yours has a special ingredient or costs less. This is your "it" factor, and you should tell all your customers!

Are you starting a business to earn money for an organization or cause that you care about? Include that in your marketing. Perhaps once your customers hear about this, they'll really want to support you and your cause. This is another "it" factor!

On a separate piece of paper, make a list of your business's "it" factors.

MY BUSINESS'S "IT" FACTORS

- My dog treats are homemade.

- They're made with all-natural ingredients—no chemicals or fillers!

- I first made these treats to give my dog something healthy to eat, and now I want to share them with others.

- These are the only locally made dog treats of their kind.

- My dog can't get enough of these treats!

- Part of my profits will go to Aliyah's Animal Shelter to help animals in need.

The list above has a few whys. Why were these dog treats made? Answer: to give a dog something healthy to eat. Why have this business besides just making money? Answer: to donate money to a local animal shelter. What are the whys on *your* list? Write them down on a separate piece of paper. This is how you create a story that will help your business stand out.

THE STORY OF MY BUSINESS

- I really like to bake, but I thought that just selling cookies or brownies wouldn't be special enough.

- I started to think about something else I'm passionate about, and that is animals. In fact, I volunteer in the local animal shelter.

- The local animal shelter, Aliyah's, doesn't have a lot of money and must sometimes turn away animals, which makes me very sad.

- When I come home from working at the shelter,

I hug my dog, Bailey, very tight. I always want to keep her safe and healthy.

- One day, I looked at the treats I was giving her. They were made with some ingredients I couldn't even pronounce, which probably means they aren't good for her. Plus, they were expensive!

- That's when I came up with the idea of a business to bake my own dog treats, with all-natural ingredients, and donate some of the profits to Aliyah's Animal Shelter.

My Why: to make healthier treats for my dog while also raising money for the local animal shelter.

....

Marketing is really just sharing your passion.
—Michael Hyatt, author

....

It is important, however, to be truthful when coming up with your marketing ideas. You can't just say something because it sounds good or you think it will attract customers. For example, if you claim you are using all-organic ingredients, you have to really do it. If you promise to donate 10 percent of your proceeds to charity, you must actually make that donation.

....

You can't sell anything if you can't tell anything.
—Beth Comstock, former CEO and vice chair,
General Electric

....

★ ★ ★ STARTUP STAR ★ ★ ★

Photo by Are You Kidding Socks

Sebastian Martinez has always loved socks. When he was six, his mom asked if he wanted to start a sock business. Sebastian grabbed paper and a pencil and started drawing. And that's how Are You Kidding Socks began!

Today, Sebastian is the CEO (also known as the boss) of the company, with older brother Brandon as the director of sales. Sebastian and Brandon have a unique story to tell—they're the only kids with their own sock company, and they donate some of their proceeds to charities like Stand Up to Cancer and Autism Speaks.

Learn more about Are You Kidding Socks at **AreYouKiddingSocks.com.**

7

BRANDING

Branding means creating a unique identity for your business.

Several things go into branding, and in this chapter we'll discuss all of them:

- a name
- a logo
- a slogan

There are a few things to keep in mind when you name your business. You want the name to be short, simple, and catchy. You might also want to try to tie the name to what you are selling. People will remember your business if you come up with a name that's easy to remember.

Let's look at some well-known businesses and how they were named:

- **Coca-Cola:** Named for the ingredients the soda was originally made from: coca leaves and kola nuts.
- **Lego:** A combination of two Danish words, *leg* and *godt*, which together mean "play well."
- **Nike:** The name of the Greek goddess of victory—the swoosh in the logo symbolizes Nike's flight.
- **Reebok:** In the Afrikaans language, *rhebok* means "antelope," an animal that is both fast and graceful.
- **Walmart:** A combination of the store's founder's name—Sam Walton—and the word *mart*, which means "store or market."
- **Wendy's:** Named after Melinda, the founder's daughter, whose nickname was Wendy.
- **Häagen-Dazs:** A totally made-up name! It's just Danish-sounding gibberish that sounded good to the ice cream brand's creators.

When brainstorming the name for your business, think about your why and your "it" factors. Can your name tie into why you started your business or what makes it stand out? The name should be easy to remember and simple to spell (although there are always exceptions, like Häagen-Dazs!). On a separate piece of paper, write down some possible names for your business.

POSSIBLE NAMES FOR MY BUSINESS

- Bark Biscuits

- Sit and Stay Biscuits

- Biscuits for a Cause

- Bailey's Homemade Dog Treats

- Bailey's Bow-Wow Biscuits

If you are having trouble coming up with a list, try brainstorming with a friend or relative. Explain your product to them. Why do you think it's special? Why would others find it special? See if your friend or relative can give you some suggestions to bounce around. Remember that when brainstorming, there are no bad ideas! Just write down every word that pops into your mind that's related to your business idea. For example, if you were coming up with a name for a business related to dogs, you can write down words like *sit, stay, roll over, fur, bark, woof, hungry, snack*. Then try combining those words in different ways.

Once you have your list, it's time to do some analyzing, like this:

POSSIBLE NAMES FOR MY BUSINESS

- **Bark Biscuits:** Will people think the biscuits are made from tree bark?

- **Sit and Stay Biscuits:** I like how this one sounds, but people might think the biscuits are only for training.

- **Biscuits for a Cause:** What kind of biscuits and what kind of cause? I don't want people to ask too many questions when they see or hear the name.

- **Bailey's Homemade Dog Treats:** Better, but a bit boring.

- **Bailey's Bow-Wow Biscuits:** I think I'm onto something here! "Bow-Wow" makes it clear that these are dog biscuits, but it's more fun than just using the word *dog*.

★ ★ ★ STARTUP STAR ★ ★ ★

When **London Miller** was nine years old, she wanted to open a lemonade business. But so many other kids were also selling lemonade; how could she put her own twist on it? London decided to make her lemonade in different flavors, such as blueberry, strawberry, cotton candy, and more. She also decided to use her name in a creative

way to make her business more personal and fun. And that was when Londonade was born. The name of this business reflects the owner and the product, and it says, "This is something unique!" You can find out more about Londonade at **MyLondonade.com**.

Whatever name you come up with for your business, make sure it's something that's uniquely *you*!

Once you decide on a name, you're ready to design a logo to go with it. A logo is an easily recognizable symbol, drawing, or picture. And just like a name, your logo should be unforgettable as well as relevant to your business. You want people to know it's your brand every time they see your logo.

For example, the three stripes in the Adidas logo represent a mountain. And it's a challenge to climb to the top of a mountain, right? So the creators of this logo might have thought that by wearing Adidas, you can meet every challenge you face!

Google

When Ruth Kedar was given the task of designing the Google logo, she was working in the primary colors: red, yellow, and blue. But to show that Google is innovative and is always pushing the boundaries, she changed the usual order of the colors and added a green l.

A good logo should be:

- simple, so people can recognize it quickly and you can reproduce it easily
- memorable, so your customers won't forget it
- timeless, so you can use it forever (don't follow the trend of the moment!)
- distinct from other businesses' logos
- appropriate for your business

Your logo can be handwritten or typewritten, colorful or black and white—whatever you like! You can design it by hand or on a phone or computer. On a separate piece of paper, try out a few logos and see which you like best.

MY LOGO IDEAS

This is my favorite logo!

You have your name and logo; now it's time to come up with a slogan. A **slogan** is a word or a phrase that attracts attention. Here are some well-known slogans to get your creative juices flowing:

- **Bounty:** the Quicker Picker Upper
- **Dunkin' Donuts:** America Runs on Dunkin'
- **M&M's:** Melts in Your Mouth, Not in Your Hand
- **Nike:** Just Do It

Each of these slogans works for a different reason. "The Quicker Picker Upper" says exactly what a good paper towel should do: clean up messes fast. "America Runs on Dunkin'" has the name of the business in the slogan, so it will stick with the customer, and "Runs on Dunkin'" refers to the energy they want people to get from consuming their coffee and donuts. When you hear "Melts in Your Mouth, Not in Your Hand," you just think of M&M's, don't you? And "Just Do It" is an inspirational slogan that makes the consumer think they can go out and do anything with a pair of Nikes on!

A good slogan will be memorable and tell your audience what your company is about. A slogan can also let your customer know what makes your product different from the competition. Why don't M&M's melt in your hand? Because they have a candy shell that protects the chocolate and prevents you from getting too messy.

STARTUP SECRET(S)

Here are a few things to consider when coming up with your slogan (and you don't have to do all of them!):

- Think of something that goes along with your product and is memorable.
- Try to include one of your product's benefits in a way that makes people feel good.
- Connect your slogan to a problem that your business solves.

On a separate piece of paper, write down some catchy slogans that fit your business, like this:

MY SLOGAN IDEAS YOU'RE THE BOSS

- Good for your dog
- Buy a biscuit, help a dog in need
- A dog's best treat
- Got treats?

Try out your slogans on your family and friends to see which one they like the best. Ask if your slogan tells them something about your business or makes them feel a certain way. Also ask if they think your slogan is memorable and catchy.

When **Reese Schroeder** was twelve years old, she started collecting gently used stuffed animals, cleaning them up, taking them apart, and sewing them into new animals. Her friends and family liked her new creations so much that she started selling them at craft fairs and online. Today, Reese's animals, called Wild and Wacky Pets, are shipped to Australia, South Korea, the United States, and the United Kingdom.

Photo by Wild and Wacky Pets

The slogan that Reese came up with for her business—Giving Homeless Stuffed Animals a New Life—tells her story in a short and catchy way. You can find out more about Reese's business at **WildAndWackyPets.wixsite.com/website**.

Great job so far! You have your business name, logo, and slogan. Now let's take a moment to check out the competition . . .

8

CHECK OUT THE COMPETITION

Chances are there's already a business like yours out there. That's okay; competition is a normal part of business. If you want to buy a pair of sneakers, for example, there are lots of brands to choose from: Nike, Reebok, Adidas, and more. If you are in the mood for a burger, which fast-food joint will you hit, McDonald's or Burger King? And if you want to send an overnight package, which delivery company will you use, UPS or FedEx?

Having competition is very important in business. It gives consumers more options. Competition forces each business to try to make their product as good as it can be. And competition ensures that prices stay level because most people won't pay a lot more money for something if they can get it for less money from another company.

Before launching your business, you want to understand your competition. What does your competition do well? For example, if you are starting a lemonade business, is your competitor successful because they set up their stand next to the park on hot days? Maybe they tell their customers an interesting story about how they started their business. Your competition also might donate some of their profits to a worthy cause. Or their product might be especially delicious.

As you are researching your competition, don't get discouraged if they are already doing some of the same things you plan to do. Now is the time to think hard about how you can put a special twist on your business. Look closely at your competition to see what they *aren't* doing. Maybe they are selling lemonade near the park, but it isn't homemade lemonade. Meanwhile *your* lemonade is homemade from a family recipe, which will make a great story!

Since you don't want to have the exact same business as someone else, look closely at what makes your product stand out from the rest. Is your product less expensive? Does it use all-natural ingredients? Perhaps your business solves your customer's problem in a better way.

On a separate piece of paper, make a list of your competitors. Write down what they do well and what they don't do well, like this:

MY COMPETITION	WHAT THEY DO WELL	WHAT THEY DON'T DO WELL
Davie's Dog Treats	They sell their treats near the dog park.	Their treats include a lot of chemicals and preservatives.
Best Dog Biscuits	They have a lot of posters around town.	Their biscuits are very expensive.
Yummie Treats	Their treats use only organic ingredients.	They don't give any of their profits to charity.

Your list will help you figure out why people might want to buy your product instead of your competitors'. How will your product be

- easier to buy?
- better value for the price?
- better?
- different?

Did you learn anything from your competition that makes you want to change aspects of your business or product to make it stand out more?

Does your competition do something poorly that you can improve upon? Could your product be more interesting? For example, maybe you plan to set up a stand to sell lemonade made with freshly squeezed lemons, water, and sugar. But that is just what everyone else in your neighborhood is doing. So what spin can you put on your lemonade? Perhaps you can add a flavor or two, such as strawberries or blueberries.

You might also discover that all the lemonade stands in your neighborhood are for profit, meaning they are keeping all the money they make for themselves. Your lemonade stand could stand out if you donate some of your profits to a charitable cause.

> *I looked at my competitors and I thought that if they could do it, I could do it. And if they are popular and doing well, I could compete with them.*
> —Tommy Hilfiger, fashion designer

There are also lessons you can learn from your competitors. Look at how they find their customers. Do they put up posters in your neighborhood? Perhaps you can do that, too. What is unique about their product? While you won't want to copy them, maybe you can be inspired by them to make your product unique as well. Taking inspiration from something is okay, but copying something exactly is not good. Think about how much time and energy you have put into your business or product. You wouldn't want someone to copy your entire idea, right?

Look at the strengths of your competitors. If a competing lemonade stand sells lots of lemonade on hot days, then you could sell your lemonade on hot days, too. However, you shouldn't set up your lemonade stand right next to your competition's stand—that wouldn't be fair. If you learned that lemonade sells well on a hot day, try to find a location where no one is selling the same product.

STARTUP SECRET

More than one company can be successful selling the same product, so don't fear the competition.

By the end of your competition research, your business will be on its way to becoming the best it can be!

9

MONEY MATTERS

One of the objectives of creating your business is to make some cash, right? So let's make sure your business will be profitable.

The first thing to consider when thinking about money is your costs, also called your **expenses**. This is the amount of money you will need to make your product and operate your business. What are all the materials you will need for your company? If you are starting a lemonade stand, for example, you will need lemons, sugar, and water. But you will also need cups to serve the lemonade and maybe napkins. These costs that you'll pay every time you make and sell lemonade are called **operating costs** because they are the costs of running—or operating—your business.

Figuring out your operating costs involves some simple

math. On a separate piece of paper, create an operating cost chart, like this:

OPERATING COSTS FOR BAILEY'S BOW-WOW BISCUITS

Ingredients	Cost per 100 Biscuits
Flour	$4.00
Peanut Butter	+ $8.00
Eggs	+ $5.00
Clear Bags and Ties	+ $3.00
Total Operating Costs	**$20.00**

Things can get a little tricky if you buy more ingredients than you need. What do you do with the leftovers? You can save them for the next batch! However, you don't want to buy too many ingredients at once because some of the items could spoil. And that would be a waste of money.

It is best to start small and then reevaluate after you have a feel for how much you are selling. If you are selling out fast, then make bigger batches. If it is taking a long time to sell out, then make smaller batches.

Now that you have figured out your operating costs, it is time to determine what you're going to charge.

It's time for some more math. On a separate piece of paper, figure out your cost per item, like this:

COST TO MAKE EACH BAG OF BAILEY'S BISCUITS

		Notes
Number of Biscuits Made per Batch	100	
Operating Costs	$20.00	Cost of ingredients + supplies
Cost per Biscuit	$0.20	($20.00 in Operating Costs divided by Number of biscuits made per batch)
Number of Biscuits per Bag	5	
Cost per Bag of Five Biscuits	$1.00	(5 biscuits times $0.20 cost per biscuit)

In this example, it costs one dollar to make each bag of treats. When figuring out what to charge your customer, try doubling what it costs you to make your product. By doing this, you would charge two dollars for each bag.

STARTUP SECRET

Your price might be very different depending on *how* you make your product, and it's not always necessary to have the lowest price. For example, homemade lemonade takes more time and money to make than lemonade from a mix, so it makes sense that you should charge more for it.

Lots of questions might be swirling through your mind at this point. Is my price too high? Is it too low? If my product costs more, how can I rationalize why? Don't worry if you have questions. You can get an idea by checking what other people are charging for the same product. If you're still not sure, just start selling, and you can always change your price later!

If instead of a product you are selling a service, such as dog-walking, you won't have much in the way of operating costs. In that case, there are a few other tools you can use to set your price. First, see what other people in your area are charging for this service. Take into consideration who the other dog walkers are. You might not be able to get the same amount of money as adult dog walkers with lots of experience, so check out what other kids your age get paid.

STARTUP SECRET

If you are starting a business to raise money for a good cause, sometimes the best price is no set price at all. When someone asks how much your product is, tell them it is pay whatever you want because all the profits go toward that cause. You might be surprised to find that people will give you more money than you would have asked for in the first place!

Also, when selling a service, think about how much your time is worth. Is it worth your time to spend a half hour walking a dog for one dollar? What else could you be doing during that time? Playing video games? Catching up on homework? How much money would you need to get paid to feel good about spending this time working rather than doing something else for no money?

In addition to your operating expenses, you may have to spend money on one-time or upfront costs to get started.

For example, if you are starting a lemonade stand, you might have to buy a lemon squeezer and a pitcher.

STARTUP SECRET

You may have to get a vendor's permit if you want to sell your product in a public place. A vendor's permit is a license to sell. Check with your local city government to find out if you need this permit and how much it costs. Some communities also want your business to have a health inspection and permits to put up signs around your neighborhood. Be sure to ask all these questions when you apply for your vendor's permit.

All these expenses are your upfront costs, or **startup costs**. Once you know your profit from each sale, figure out how long it will take to earn back your upfront costs. Once you've earned back your upfront costs, then you are really making money!

On a separate piece of paper, figure out how many items you need to sell to earn back your upfront costs, like this:

HOW MUCH I NEED TO SELL TO BREAK EVEN

Price per Item	$2.00
Minus Cost per Item	($1.00)
Equals Profit per Item	$1.00
Upfront Costs *(shaped biscuit cutters and poster board and markers to advertise)*	$10.00
Divided by Profit per Item	$1.00
Equals Number of Items to Sell to Earn Back Upfront Costs	10

STARTUP SECRET

Starting a business might cost you some money you don't have. Maybe you can ask a parent, grandparent, or other adult for a loan with the promise to repay it within a certain amount of time. (If you do this, make sure you actually do repay the loan!) Or you can try doing some one-time jobs, such as raking leaves, babysitting, or helping with extra chores around the house to make the needed cash.

If you're having trouble figuring out your costs or prices, ask a friend, relative, or teacher to help!

Once you set your price, remember that it is not set in stone. It is okay to raise or even lower your price. You might have to raise your price if your costs go up. And you might have to lower your price if people seem interested in your product but walk away when they hear how much it costs.

The goal is to set a fair price: one that makes your customers happy enough to come back for more, and one that will make you a profit.

10
PERFECTING YOUR PITCH

Y ou can use parts of your story to help formulate your sales pitch. A sales pitch is a few short sentences that get people interested in your business. It's also called an elevator pitch because it should be brief enough that you can say it in the time it takes to ride an elevator—and skyscrapers don't count!

Your pitch should answer some of the following questions:

- What is your business? Explain what you're selling.
- What problem does your business help solve, and how?
- What makes your product or idea stand out from all the rest? Make sure your pitch includes your why!
- Will your business benefit a cause or charity?

The language you use in your sales pitch is important. You might

- ask a question
- tell a story
- use humor
- be sincere

On a separate piece of paper, write down your sales pitch, like this:

MY SALES PITCH

Hi! I'm the owner of Bailey's Bow-Wow Biscuits. Do you want a treat that is healthy for your dog, made only from delicious all-natural ingredients? Well, these biscuits are just what you need! I created them for my dog, Bailey, and she just gobbles them up! Part of the proceeds goes to Aliyah's Animal Shelter.

The above pitch is good because it

- introduces the name of the business ("Bailey's Bow-Wow Biscuits")
- asks a question ("Do you want a treat that is healthy for your dog?")

- says what makes this product special ("all-natural ingredients")
- tells a story ("I created them for my dog, Bailey, and she just gobbles them up!")
- mentions that part of the proceeds goes to a good cause ("Part of the proceeds goes to Aliyah's Animal Shelter.")

Not every pitch can answer *all* the questions, but try to answer as many as possible while keeping your pitch short.

Writing down your pitch is a good first step. Next, practice saying it aloud. You want to deliver your pitch with enthusiasm and passion. If you simply read your pitch without emotion, you might end up putting your potential customer to sleep!

Lots of people tend to feel a bit shy talking to people they don't know, so don't worry if you have this feeling. It's easier to talk to people if you know exactly what you are going to say. So it might be easier if you think of your pitch like memorizing lines in a school play. And just like a school play, make sure to deliver your lines with a lot of feeling!

Practice your pitch in front of a mirror, your family, and your friends. As you are speaking, put emphasis on important words. Use some hand gestures and facial expressions. Throughout your pitch, try to change the tone of your voice and the speed at which you speak, but try not to talk too quickly. And always try to look your customer in the eyes, with a smile on your face. It's rehearsed, but you want it to sound natural.

Act enthusiastic and you will be enthusiastic.

—Dale Carnegie, motivational speaker

As you practice, take note of the reactions you get. Does your audience seem as excited as you? Do they understand what you are selling? Are you able to convince them to buy your product or service?

If you don't get a satisfactory reaction to your pitch, you may need to refine it. Perhaps it's too long. Maybe you're speaking too slowly and in a boring manner—or too fast, and they can't understand you. Remember that even though this is the hundredth time you've said (and heard!) your pitch, it's the first time your customer is hearing it, so try to be enthusiastic every time.

A good pitch is creative and uses descriptive language:

- Instead of saying "I am selling some lemonade," you can say, "I am selling ice-cold, refreshing lemonade."
- Instead of saying "Is your dog alone during the day?

Maybe I can walk him," try saying "Are you afraid that your dog is lonely being home alone all day? Then I can walk him, and we can have some fun together!"

- Instead of saying "I'm selling Bonnie's Bows," you can say, "I'm selling Bonnie's Bows, which will make your hair look bow-u-tiful!"

STARTUP SECRET

Go back and look at your slogan. Can you use all or part of it in your sales pitch?

Rehearse your sales pitch enough that you are comfortable pitching your business to anyone, anywhere, at any time. You never know when you might meet a potential customer!

11

CUSTOMER RESEARCH

How will you make sure people will want your product or service? While you can never be 100 percent certain, you can take some steps to be *pretty* confident that people will want what you are selling.

The first thing you should do is test your product. Make a couple of samples and give them to your friends and family for free. The first products you make to try out your business are called **prototypes**. Ask your testers to be totally honest with you about the product. Although it might hurt your feelings if you hear something negative, try not to take the comments personally. Remember, the comments are not about *you*, they are about your product. Feedback can help make your product better. On a separate piece of paper, make a list of who you want to be your testers, like this:

MY TESTERS

my dog

my neighbor's dog

I will also give samples to our vet and the
local pet store and ask for feedback.

Think up specific questions to ask your testers. If you ask everyone the same questions, you can compare their answers and see what your testers agree needs to change or is working well. You might even want to create a list of questions you can ask your testers or a little survey that they can complete and return to you. On a separate piece of paper, create a survey or questions that you want to ask, like this:

BAILEY'S BOW-WOW BISCUITS—SURVEY

Thank you for being willing to have your dog test my biscuits. After your dog has eaten some, please fill out this survey and return it to me.

1. Did your dog eat the biscuit or spit it out?

2. Did your dog like the biscuit? Did your dog ask/ beg for another one?

3. How much would you pay for a biscuit like this?

4. Can you describe how you feel about the ingredients?

5. Would you choose this biscuit over a competitor? Why or why not?

6. Would you recommend these biscuits to your friends? Why or why not?

7. On a scale of 1–5, with 5 being the best score, how would you rate the biscuits?

8. Is there anything I can do to improve the biscuits?

Once you get back your surveys, you can compare the answers. Do many people think that your price is too high? Then you might want to consider lowering it. Is there an ingredient that you can add or take away to make your product better? Try not to get upset or discouraged by the feedback—instead, use it as a tool to make your business better.

You should also test out your company name, logo, and slogan. Ask your potential customers if your name and logo are good fits with your product. This is a good time to try your sales pitch again, too. Any tweaks that you can make as a result of the feedback will only improve your overall business.

If you feel more comfortable doing your initial testing on

your friends and family, that's totally okay. But it is a good idea to test your product on people who are in your target audience. This will give you an idea of how your product will be received by the people you think will buy it.

For example, if you are setting up a lemonade stand, try giving out free lemonade samples on a hot day to kids who just finished playing sports. They will be thirsty for sure and will be willing testers! With each cup of lemonade you can hand out your survey. Or you could just ask a few simple questions:

- Was the lemonade too sweet or not sweet enough?
- If I charged $1.00 per cup, would you buy it? Why or why not?
- Is there anything I can do to improve my lemonade?

Each time you test your product, be sure to introduce your business, be friendly, and tell your potential customer when and where you plan to open your shop. That way, if they like it, they'll know how to come back for more!

12
SPREAD THE WORD

Your friends, family, and product testers know about your business, but you are going to need more customers than that to have a successful business. Now is the time to spread the word about your company and put your marketing plan into action. A marketing plan is a list of how you will get people interested in your business.

There are many ways in which your marketing can tell people about your business:

- social media
- signs, posters, and flyers
- postcards
- email
- word of mouth
- advertising (which is when you pay to show your marketing)

If you want to use social media, like TikTok, Instagram, or Twitter, you first must be old enough and have an adult's permission to post on these platforms. If you are not old enough or not allowed to, perhaps an older person like a parent, guardian, or grandparent can make the posts for you.

Consider your target customers' behaviors and activities so you can best reach them through your marketing. Do your customers shop at certain stores? For example, if you're starting a lemonade stand, you could put up flyers or posters in or around the park. Always be sure to get permission before promoting your business.

On a separate piece of paper, make a list of how you will tell people about your business, like this:

MY MARKETING IDEAS

Ask the vet if I can leave some flyers in her office waiting room.

Hand out flyers at the dog park.

Make some posters and ask the pet stores if I can hang them in their windows.

Ask my mom for the email addresses of her friends with dogs and send them emails.

Text my friends who are dog owners.

Just like your sales pitch, keep your ads short, attention-getting, and creative so people will remember them. Come up with a slogan that people won't forget. Think about advertising that you have seen online, on social media, or on TV that you just can't get out of your mind. Go back and look at the slogan you created for your business. If it is short and catchy, you may want to use that in your marketing.

On a separate piece of paper, create a flyer for your product or business, like this:

MY FLYER

BAILEY'S BOW-WOW

A DOG'S BEST TREAT

All-natural and yummy!
Only $2.00 for 5 drool-inducing treats.

Your dog will eat them up!

STARTUP SECRET

There's something in marketing called the Rule of Seven, which says that someone needs to see or hear your marketing message at least seven times before they buy from you. So, don't be afraid to create *a lot* of ads!

Sometimes the best form of marketing is word of mouth. This means that someone hears about your business and they tell a friend about it, who tells a friend, and they tell a friend . . . You get the point. But for anyone to tell someone else about your business, they must be happy with your product or service. So the absolute most important thing is to deliver a good product and to do so in a friendly way. After a customer has made a purchase, don't be shy about asking them to recommend your business to a friend!

13
READY FOR LAUNCH!

Where you sell your product is very, very important. If you sell in the wrong place, you won't make any money. In fact, there's a saying that the three most important things in business are location, location, and location! When deciding where to set up, think about how easily you will be able to reach your target audience from your location. Also consider *when* you are selling your product. If you set up your refreshing, ice-cold lemonade stand during a snowstorm, do you think you will have many buyers?

You might have to ask permission to set up somewhere other than your own stoop or lawn. For example, if you want to sell lemonade right outside a supermarket, you will have to ask permission from the supermarket owner.

Once you know your location, think about how to display your product. This is called **merchandising**. Just setting up a plain table with a pitcher and paper cups isn't going to attract as many customers as setting up a decorated table with an attention-grabbing sign. Think razzle and dazzle and bling! On a separate piece of paper, write down some ideas about how you will merchandise your product, like this:

MY MERCHANDISING IDEAS

1. Buy or make a tablecloth with pictures of dogs and dog bones.

2. Create a colorful sign with the name of my business.

3. Tie bright ribbons around the dog biscuit bags.

4. Stack the dog biscuit bags in a cute way.

Although it is great to decorate your stand in a fancy way, or to create eye-catching signs, you need to remember that your merchandising costs are part of your startup costs. So, think about how much your merchandising will cost and how many more units of your product you will have to make, or how many more hours of your service you will have to provide, to make a profit. You might want to start small with your merchandising. For example, making a sign with flourescent markers is a lot less expensive than making one that lights up!

★ ★ ★ **STARTUP STAR** ★ ★ ★

Eric Vasquez started playing with LEGO® bricks when he was two years old. By the time he was nine, he was selling the toys from a folding table at sidewalk sales and markets. He used his profits to start his very own physical store, Connect the Brick, in Tacoma, Washington. His shop has a bright, welcoming storefront, and inside are floor-to-ceiling shelves filled

Photo by Tony Vasquez

with hundreds of LEGO® products. He also sells toys from his website, **ConnectTheBrick.com**.

You can also set up a website for your business. Having a website allows you to attract a wider network of customers. You can refer people to your website to learn more about your business, product, or service. If you are not old enough, or not allowed to use the internet, ask an adult to help. Building a website isn't as tough as it might sound, and there are plenty of hosting sites and platforms that make it even easier.

When looking for the best platform to use, you will want something with a lot of templates. A **template** is a pattern or a guide that is provided for you so you don't have to create your own from scratch. You will also want a hosting site that has fun images and designs that you can use. If you don't want to spend a lot of money, or any at all, look for a company that offers these services for free.

If you do create a website, be sure to include your website's information in all of your marketing. And if you spend any money on designing or hosting your website, make sure to track that in your list of startup costs.

★ ★ ★ **STARTUP STAR** ★ ★ ★

Zori Thomas (aka Jammy Girl) started her business, Soap and Soothe by Jammy Girl, when she was eleven years old. She had a learning disability and severe anxiety,

Photo by Ward Creative Studios

and she wanted an outlet where she could focus her thoughts and cope with her challenges. She started making sweet-smelling soaps and soon wanted to turn this into a business. At first her mom said no, but when Zori proved she could be responsible enough to run a business, her mom hopped on board. Zori is also a proud advocate for adoption. She wrote these inspiring words: "After more than five years of living out my dream, I have had the opportunity to and want to continue to inspire others. Those who perhaps didn't get off to a great start in life. Those who struggle with the day-to-day. Those who were chosen by their parents."

You don't need to create your own website to sell your product online. Sites such as Zazzle and Etsy allow you to sell your own goods using their platforms. The upside of these sites is that you can easily display your products to a very large audience. The downside of these sites, however, is that you don't get to keep all of your profits like you would if you sold in person. (They take a percentage of whatever you make.) You might want to consider selling on these sites *and* in person.

Another easy way to start a business is by creating a

social media account for your business and taking orders by direct message. It's a lot faster and easier than setting up a website and allows you to get some quick feedback (and orders!) before you spend the time to make a website.

Whether you create your own website, sell through an online store, or set up an in-person stand, you can run special promotions for your customers, like buy two and get one free, or buy two and get one at half price. These promotions are useful ways to jump-start sales or attract new customers. And if you are donating part of your profits to a charity, be sure to say so wherever you are selling!

When you're setting up your stand, make sure you have everything you need. If you have a lemonade stand, bring the lemonade, pitchers, and cups, of course. But what will happen if you sell out early? Will you have the supplies with you to make more lemonade? Or will there be someone with you who can run back home to make some more? What if it's a windy day and your signs are flapping around? Bring some tape with you. And where will you put the money from your sales? Will you have a cashbox or a jar? And what if you need to make change? Be sure to have plenty of coins and dollar bills. Try to anticipate issues that might come up. And make note of what you've forgotten this time, so that next time you can be even more prepared.

On your first day of business, make sure you start off on the right foot. Don't bring too much product with you or else you will have to haul all the extras back home or throw them out if it's something that could spoil. It is better to have too little than too much on your first day to avoid waste.

If people are looking at your product and not buying, ask them (in a polite way) why not. Is it the price? The ingredients? Just like when you were doing your testing, don't get discouraged by their answers. What they tell you can only make your product better!

STARTUP SECRET

Ask your customers or passersby if there is anything else they would be interested in purchasing. You might get an idea for something to add to your current business or an idea for your next business!

When speaking with your customers, be sure to smile, make eye contact, and be polite. Even if someone doesn't buy, always thank them for looking. They might not have been your customer today, but maybe tomorrow they will be, so always be courteous. If someone does buy, thank them, and if you have their contact information, send a thank-you note and ask them to refer your business to their friends. Make your customers feel good about buying from you and they'll want to come back.

································

I've learned that people will forget what you said,
people will forget what you did, but people will
never forget how you made them feel.

—Maya Angelou, author

································

It is always a good idea to follow up with your customers. While this may be easier to do with customers who purchase something from you online, you could keep a notepad on your stand and ask customers (or even browsers) to jot down their names and emails or phone numbers. This way you can send them information on where you'll be selling next, if you have added new products, or when you are running specials.

STARTUP SECRET

It's often easier to sell more to an existing customer than it is to find a new customer.

If you are selling a service, such as dog-walking or babysitting, you can still do some merchandising. Perhaps you can set up a table with flyers advertising your business. In the same way as if you were selling a product, make your table fun and eye-catching.

The more creative you are, the more customers you will attract!

14

BALANCING YOUR TIME AND MONEY

I t's a fact that as a business owner, you will work hard. And chances are, you will have to balance your business responsibilities with your schoolwork, volunteering, leisure time, sports or band practice, and everything else going on in your life. This is where **time management** comes in. Try to figure out the right amount of time to devote to each activity so you can get it all done (without getting stressed out!). One idea is to use a daily planner. In your planner, you can block out a section of time for each task.

To make a schedule, you need a rough sense of how long things will take. On a separate piece of paper, write down a weekly schedule that includes everything you have to do, like this:

MY WEEKLY

	MONDAY	TUESDAY	WEDNESDAY
7:00	wake up	wake up	wake up
8:00	school	school	school
9:00			
10:00			
11:00			
12:00			
1:00			
2:00			
3:00	homework	soccer practice	homework
4:00			
5:00	work on business	work on business	work on business
6:00	dinner	dinner	dinner
7:00	homework	homework	homework
8:00			
9:00	get ready for bed	get ready for bed	get ready for bed
10:00			

SCHEDULE

YOU'RE THE BOSS

THURSDAY	FRIDAY	SATURDAY	SUNDAY
wake up	wake up	wake up	wake up
school	school	soccer	do chores
			selling time
		selling time	
		lunch break	lunch break
		selling time	selling time
soccer practice	hang out with friends		
		hang out with friends	hang out with friends
dinner	dinner	dinner	dinner
homework	homework		
		read/free time	homework/ read/free time
get ready for bed	get ready for bed	get ready for bed	get ready for bed

Your schedule might change each week, so it's a good idea to create weekly schedules in a notebook or a planner.

Besides managing your time, it is also important to manage your money. Keep a record of every dollar you make and spend on your business. Sometimes you may see your profits go up, which is good. But if you see your profits go down, you need to figure out why. Has the cost of ingredients or supplies gone up? If so, you may need to consider raising your prices. Or perhaps you have been busy with other things and haven't spent much time looking for customers. Figuring out why your profits are down will help you get back on track.

STARTUP SECRET

Here are three words that you need to know when running a business:

- **Revenue** is the money a customer pays you for your product or service.
- **Expense** is the money you spend to run your business.
- **Profit** is the amount of money that is left over after you have paid all your costs. In other words, it's your Revenue minus your Expenses.

Now we come to a word that you've probably heard a lot of adults say they don't like: taxes. When it comes to taxes, kids must follow the same rules as adults. The rules are complicated, but they boil down to this: if you earn more than a certain amount each year, you must pay some percentage of your profits to the government in taxes. You might even have to collect sales tax from your customers on each item they purchase. For this part of your business, it's best to ask an adult for help so you're paying the correct amount of taxes and at the right time.

When running a business, it's important to keep track of the number of products you sell each day. This way, you will know how frequently to make more product or if you have too much. The same goes for the materials or ingredients you use to make your product. If you run out of something, you won't be able to make your product, which means lost sales. Keep a careful record of all the materials you have on hand so you'll know when to buy more. Make sure to jot down where you operated your business, what day of the week and time of day, what the weather was, and anything else that you think might have had an impact on your sales that day so you know for next time.

MY WEEKLY SALES

Day	Location	Bags Sold	Price per Bag	Revenue	Cost to Make Each Bag	Expenses	Profit (Revenue minus Expenses)
Monday	My house	2	$2.00	$4.00	$1.00	$2.00	$2.00
Tuesday	My house	2	$2.00	$4.00	$1.00	$2.00	$2.00
Thursday	My house	0	$2.00	—	$1.00	—	—
Saturday	Soccer field	8	$2.00	$16.00	$1.00	$8.00	$8.00
Sunday	Town fair	6	$2.00	$12.00	$1.00	$6.00	$6.00
Total for Week		18		$36.00		$18.00	$18.00

Notes: I sold 20 bags, so that means I sold 100 biscuits (20 bags x 5 biscuits per bag).

I sold out my first batch of 100 biscuits—time to bake more! I still have enough ingredients for another batch, so I don't have any additional expenses.

In addition, keep a careful record of your customers, with their names and contact information. You might also want to make some notes about them. For example, if you have a babysitting business, keep a record what time the kids go to bed, what types of games they like to play, what they can and cannot eat, and so on. Or if you sell lemonade, make a note of which customers like their lemonade with ice and which customers prefer it without ice.

MY CUSTOMERS

Day	Place Sold	Customer Name
Monday	My house	Lauren B. (1 bag) email: LaurenBGood@coldmail.com Has a goldendoodle named Dallas
Saturday	Near the soccer field	Timothy E. (2 bags) email: orangutim@normalemail.com His Pomeranian is allergic to grass
	Near the soccer field	Robin G. (2 bags) email: RobinDaBank@mailmail.com Looking for ideas for her dog's third birthday
Sunday	At the town fair	Kathy M. (1 bag) email: ItsRainingKatsAndDogs@fakemail.com Interested in cat treats, too!

Notes: Call or email customers next week to see how their dogs liked the biscuits.

It got quiet in the afternoon when I sold near the soccer field, so next time I can leave a little earlier.

It was rainy on Monday, so there weren't as many people outside my house as usual.

Managing your time and money are important skills to master not only for your business, but for your everyday life, too!

★ ★ ★ STARTUP STAR ★ ★ ★

When **Moziah Bridges** was nine years old, he wanted an accessory to help him look sharp. His grandmother helped him make his own bow tie. And it was *stylish*! Right there, at his grandmother's kitchen table, his business, Mo's Bows, was born.

Today, Mo's Bows is an internationally recognized brand. As a successful entrepreneur, Mo has sometimes found it hard to balance his business with his schoolwork and other commitments, so he relies on his BOWS of Business: **B**elieve in yourself, take the **O**pportunity to give back, **W**ork hard/study hard, and have **S**upport from friends and family.

Learn more about Mo's Bows at **MosBowsMemphis.com**.

photo by Annabella Charles Photography

15

YOU GOTTA HAVE GRIT!

Entrepreneurs are comfortable with risk and even with failure. Have you ever heard the expression "Win some, lose some"? Well, entrepreneurs don't say that. They know that even if their business fails, they haven't really lost— instead, they've learned something that will help their next business succeed. Entrepreneurs say, "Win some, learn some."

What does that mean for you? It means that if your business isn't successful, try again. You might have to make changes to your existing business based on what you learned. You might even have to start a new business. But no matter what, don't give up! One of the most impor- tant qualities an entrepreneur needs is **grit**.

Grit is having the ability to keep working toward a goal even when it's hard. Think back to your original goal when you started your business. Was it to make money to buy something special? Did you want to make money to contribute to a charity or cause? Was your business started to solve a problem? Did it have something to do with what you are passionate about? Toss these reasons around in your mind. Are they still important to you? Yes!

Some businesses are successful right away, but plenty aren't. If you find yourself in a situation where your business isn't flourishing, know that you're not alone and this chapter is for you.

There are lots of reasons why businesses don't succeed:

1. The price was too high, and not enough people wanted to buy the product or service.

2. The price was too low, and the business couldn't make a profit.

3. There was too much competition, and the product or service didn't stand out.

4. There was too little marketing, so not enough people knew about the business.

5. Customers weren't attracted by the business's sales pitch.

6. The business wasn't able to get people to buy more than once or to get them to recommend the business to their friends.

7. Your friends and family loved your product, but

there weren't enough other people who did, too.

8. Running a successful business took more time than you had to devote to it.

9. Too much product was left over and had to be thrown away, so the business lost money.

10. The business needed more money to buy more supplies.

Look carefully at this list and, on a separate piece of paper, make your own list of things you could have done differently to help your business succeed. Next to it, make a list of things that worked well in your business.

TAKING STOCK OF MY BUSINESS

WHAT WORKED WELL

Many customers who bought biscuits came back for seconds.

People liked my business's name and logo.

Dogs liked the treats!

WHAT DIDN'T WORK WELL

Not enough people found out about my business.

Making and packaging the biscuits took much more time than I'd expected.

Many passersby didn't carry cash.

After making your lists, it's decision time. Can you make changes to improve your business? If you make these changes, do you think your business will succeed? It's okay if the answer to this question is no—gather your grit and start another business! The good news is that you don't have to start from scratch: you've done a lot of the work already. Go back and look at some of the lists you first made when you were brainstorming ideas. What other passions, interests, and skills did you write down? Can you turn another one of them into a business? Of course you can! Remember that you can always find opportunity in failure. Win some, learn some!

Don't be discouraged if your business doesn't succeed. In fact, there are lots of famous entrepreneurs who had to restart their businesses or create new ones.

Walt Disney created the character Oswald the Lucky Rabbit in 1927. Disney produced twenty-seven cartoons starring this goofy rabbit, but then the rights were taken away. This meant that Disney could no longer create Oswald cartoons, and the company lost a lot of money. But instead of giving up, Disney scraped together some money and produced the film *Snow White and the Seven Dwarfs*. The movie was *huge*, and Disney became an enormous success!

You may not realize it when it happens,
but a kick in the teeth may be the best thing
in the world for you.

—Walt Disney

Today, Arianna Huffington is known as a successful author and publisher. But that wasn't always the case. After she published her first book, she had a very hard time getting her next one published. In fact, she was rejected by thirty-six publishers! But Huffington didn't give up. She tried and tried until she found a publisher. And when she started her own online newspaper, the *Huffington Post*, many critics didn't like it and thought it would never succeed. But it did and went on to have millions and millions of readers!

We need to accept that we won't always make
the right decisions, that we'll screw up royally
sometimes—understanding that failure is not the
opposite of success, it's part of success.

—Arianna Huffington, founder and CEO,

Thrive Global

It's important to realize that even very successful people don't always succeed. Twelve-year-old Beyoncé's singing and dance group was defeated on the television talent show *Star Search*. Anna Wintour was fired from the magazine *Harper's Bazaar* and then bounced back to become the head of *Vogue*. Actress Kerry Washington was cut from two television pilots before landing the leading role in the television show *Scandal*. And Oprah Winfrey was fired from her first job as television anchor!

Thinking like an entrepreneur means getting comfortable taking risks. It means trying things even though you don't know how they will turn out. Think about the first time you tried a new video game, gymnastics move, or dance routine. You took a risk. It was probably hard at first, and maybe you failed, but you learned from your failure and got better and better at it by trying again. Of course some risks (like crossing the street without looking both ways) are dangerous and not worth trying. But others (like auditioning for a play, starting a challenging book, trying a new food, or launching a new business) could be fun and worthwhile, even if they don't always turn out the way you had hoped.

Taking a risk will build your confidence.

You can learn a new skill from taking a risk.

You can improve something about yourself by taking a risk.

Taking a risk can make you happy.

....

If you take a risk and it doesn't go as planned, welcome to the club.

—Fran Hauser, startup investor and advisor

....

Not all businesses succeed. Others succeed just for a little while. And that's okay! It doesn't mean that you're a failure or that you had a bad idea. You tried something new. You had fun. Maybe you made something that you're proud of, and maybe you even earned some money. You definitely learned things that will help your next business succeed.

The important thing is that you took a risk and went after your dreams. And next time, you'll be wiser, stronger, and more likely to make your business a *huge* success as the Comeback Kid. Win some, learn some!

16
BUILDING YOUR EMPIRE

Simone Bridges was just three years old when her grandmother taught her how to bake. She was immediately hooked! Simone practiced her baking skills and put her unique spin on everything she learned from her grandmother. At nine, Simone began selling her homemade treats to her church family, neighbors, and friends. And at the age of eleven, Simone opened her own business: Goddess Food Factory.

Since 2017, Simone's treats have received rave reviews from people around the world, including celebrities and master chefs, and Goddess Food Factory now has several employees. But Simone's passion didn't start and end with baking—Simone is also committed to STREAM education (science, technology, reading, engineering, arts, math). So she combined her two passions and now teaches STREAM concepts through her hands-on cooking classes. As a STREAM advocate, Simone serves her community and youth worldwide by providing education on cooking basics, STREAM, and how to become a kid entrepreneur. Plus, she has her own nonprofit organization, Simone Bridges Inspires, Inc. You can learn more about Simone and shop her products at GoddessFoodFactory.com.

Photo by Paul Stewart Photography

It is possible for you, too, to build an empire after you succeed, just like Simone! If your business is going well, you may want to consider hiring employees. Who will you hire? Your employee (or employees) should be interested in your business. After all, if they aren't interested, they won't be good salespeople or workers, right? So you should create a clear job description to help ensure you are hiring the right person.

HELP WANTED

- Do you love to bake?
- Do you love dogs?
- Do you love both?

- Then Bailey's Bow-Wow Biscuits wants to talk to you about working for us!

- We are looking for people between the ages of 14 and 17 to work 2-6 hours per week, baking and selling dog biscuits.

- If you are interested, please call 555-BARK.

Be sure to figure out how much you will pay an employee and if you can afford to hire them before starting the hiring process. On the one hand, paying employees will increase your operating expenses. On the other hand, having two people selling or making your product instead of just one might increase your revenue and profits so much that it's worth it!

STARTUP SECRET

Most states require that employees are at least fourteen years old. Try to find your state's age requirement by searching online for a phrase like: "How old do you have to be to work in [state's name]?" and then show your research to an adult.

When interviewing potential employees, always be friendly and clearly explain your business and the role you're trying to fill. During the interview, you want to determine whether the person is a good fit for your business. Are they interested in what you do? Do you think they will interact well with your customers? Are they trustworthy and responsible? Can they put you in touch with some people who might recommend them for this job?

STARTUP SECRET

What happens if your business gets too big to run from your home? Check out some local commercial kitchens or manufacturing locations that can provide you more space to operate and help your business grow. Much like hiring employees, it will cost more money—but it could also make it possible for you to *earn* more money!

Once your business is up and running, you might consider adding more products to your brand, just like Cory did when he added different flavors to his cookie business. Those new products are called **brand extensions**. This is another strategy for growing your business. So if your customers loved your peanut butter–flavored dog treats, try experimenting with sweet potato treats. The dogs might gobble those up, too!

Once your business is profitable, you should figure out what to do with the money you make. Think about the Three S's:

- Save some—open a savings account
- Share some—donate to a good cause
- Spend some—invest in your business or buy something you always wanted

On a separate piece of paper, plan how to split up your profits, like this:

WHAT I WILL DO WITH MY $$$ (MY FIRST $60.00)

Save Some	Share Some	Spend Some
$20.00 for college	$20.00 for the animal shelter	$20.00: $10.00 for more supplies, $10.00 for that shirt I saw in the mall

When saving money, you might want to put it somewhere other than your piggy bank or under your mattress. Many banks and credit unions will let kids open an account.

There are different reasons to put some money aside: you might want to save up for something that's really expensive, put away money for college, or buy a gift for someone. Whatever your reason, a bank or credit union is a great place to keep your money safe.

You can share some of your profits with a charity or nonprofit organization, or you can use some of that money to invest in the businesses of other kids who want to become entrepreneurs. You can also be a mentor to kids who are just starting out and teach them some of the things that you learned while running your business.

Spending more money on your business, like buying additional supplies or advertising, is something else you can use your profits for. And remember, there is nothing wrong with spending some money on yourself. After all, you've earned it!

Now it's time for the congratulations:

CONGRATULATIONS! You found your passion and idea for your business.

CONGRATULATIONS! You identified your target audience.

CONGRATULATIONS! You created a
marketing plan.

CONGRATULATIONS! Your business
has a name, slogan, and logo.

CONGRATULATIONS! You developed
and perfected your sales pitch.

CONGRATULATIONS! You checked
out the competition and did your
consumer research.

CONGRATULATIONS! You know all
about money.

CONGRATULATIONS! You stuck
with it! You did it!

CONGRATULATIONS! You learned
how to think like an entrepreneur!

Starting and maintaining a business is hard work. But
it's rewarding work, too. As cosmetics founder Mary Kay

Ash said, "Don't limit yourself. Many people limit themselves to what they think they can do. You can go as far as your mind lets you. What you believe, remember, you achieve."

So,

Ready,

Set,

LAUNCH!

BAILEY'S BOW-WOW

Dog Biscuit Recipe

Ava Dorsey has been passionate about making treats for dogs and cats, with all-natural, healthy ingredients, since she was eight years old. That was when she came up with her first business plan for her company, Ava's Pet Palace. Today, Ava's Pet Palace treats are sold in hundreds of stores all over the United States. Learn more at AvasPetPalace.com.

Ava is always in the kitchen, experimenting with new recipes. Here's one you can try (with the help of an adult!):

INGREDIENTS

1 1/4 cup brown rice flour

1 1/4 cup oat flour

1 banana

1 cup oats

1 egg

1/2 cup water

1 teaspoon cinnamon

PREPARATION

Mix all ingredients into a dough. Once the dough is ready, you can either roll the dough and cookie-cut it into whatever fun shapes you want, or you can make balls that are about 3/4 of an inch wide. Place on a baking sheet and bake for 25–30 minutes at 350 degrees Fahrenheit. (**ALWAYS ASK AN ADULT FOR HELP WHEN USING THE OVEN**.) Let the treats cool completely before feeding them to your furry friends!